INTERMITTENT FASTING FOR BEGINNERS

The Ultimate Weight Loss Guide incl. 5 2 Diet, 16 8 Diet and 30 Days Diet Plan

1st Edition

Sarah Amber Patterson

ISBN- 9781093349689

TABLE OF CONTENTS

What Is Intermittent Fasting? 1

How Does Intermittent Fasting Work? 9

The Different Fasting Methods 17

The 16:8 Method 19

The 5:2 Method 23

30 Day Weight-Loss Plan 27

    Banana Yogurt Crunch 30

    Bacon and Tomato Poached Eggs 32

    Tropical Green Smoothie 34

    Mushroom and Garlic Frittata 37

    Italian Omelet 41

    Cinnamon Pear Porridge 44

Yogurt with Berries..46

Mushroom Delight...48

Baked Moroccan Eggs..50

Hot Chicken Salad...54

Cozy Vegetable Soup...57

Roasted Vegetables with Chermoula Tofu.................................60

Flageolet Bean and Lamb Stew...63

Coriander and Chili Fish Parcel..66

Zucchini Tagliatelle with Italian Meatballs..............................68

Ginger and Soy Sauce Stir-Fried Pork.....................................71

Garlic and Tomato Shrimp...74

Stuffed Mushrooms...77

Rice Cake Caprese..79

Pesto Tuna Salad..81

Salmon and Tabbouleh Bowl..84

Green Soup with Halloumi Croutons.......................................88

Chorizo, Chicken and Avocado Salad......................................92

Disclaimer 97

Imprint 99

What Is Intermittent Fasting?

Intermittent fasting is a popular wellness and diet trend that is taking the world by storm. Fasting is abstaining from food, drink, or both for a predetermined amount of time, ranging fromhours to days. Intermittent fasting is a pattern of eating that cycles periods of eating and fasting, or not eating. Research shows that adopting an eating plan that includes intermittent fasting helps control or lose weight, prevent some diseases, improve metabolism, and more. While diets revolve around what or how much you can eat, intermittent fasting instead centers around the timing of meals and snacks. Intermittent fasting, when done properly, is not just a diet plan, it's a way of life.

Why do people fast?

Fasting has been practiced for thousands of years. There are many different reasons for fasting, and they are not always intentional. You fast every day, whether you realize it or not. The word "breakfast" refers to the morning meal, when people break their fast after sleeping through the night. You are already practicing fasting if you follow the general meal guidelines of breakfast, lunch, and dinner. If you wait until later in the morning to eat your breakfast, you have extended your fast.

Lack of resources

Sometimes people have been forced to fast due to famine, financial depression, limited access to food, or any reason why they could not eat that was not a choice.

Weight management

Many people use different variations of fasting to maintain or lose weight. No matter which method of fasting you choose, fasting helps reduce your calorie intake and boost your metabolism, resulting in weight loss.

Self-control

Intermittent fasting, like any diet plan, requires self-control over meal habits, so some may use fasting simply as a way to exercise self-control.

Religion

Religious traditions such as Buddhism, Islam, and Christianity require periods of fasting. The purpose is usually to take the practitioner's mind off of food or any other earthly attachments and focus solely on a higher power. Fasting could also be used as a form of penance for sins in some religions.

Illness

Animals and humans instinctively fast during illness. There is an old saying, "feed a cold, starve a fever." This means the body needs more calories to cure a cold, but you should fast to reduce a fever. Despite this common saying, people are torn on whether you should eat to fuel your body and fight an infection, or that avoiding eating helps the body heal an infection more quickly. Many believe that the naturally suppressed appetite you experience at the beginning of an infection is the body's way of fighting infection to heal itself

Fasting affects the immune system by forcing the body to depend on its energy stores to maintain normal functions. The first store the body relies on is glucose, which is primarily found in the form of glycogen in your muscles and liver. The body typically runs out of glucose to use after one or two days. Then the body will resort to using fat and muscle protein for energy.

Using a lot of fat for fuel causes the body to produce ketones, which the brain and body can then use as an energy source. The ketone beta-hydroxybutyrate (BHB) is believed to boost the body's immune system. Research shows that exposing human immune cells to beta-hydroxybutyrate in amounts comparable to those found in the human body after a couple days of fasting reduced inflammation. Research also revealed that fasting for a two to three-day period can boost the recycling of damaged immune cells, enabling the regeneration of healthy new immune cells.

Cold and flu infections are caused either by bacteria or viruses (such as the influenza virus and rhinovirus). Infection from these viruses lowers the body's ability to defend itself against bacteria, increasing the likelihood of contracting a simultaneous bacterial infection with similar symptoms to the original illness.

There are three hypotheses as to why the body may naturally suppress the appetite in order to fight infection:

1. Not being hungry negates the desire to search for and prepare food. When you think about animals in nature, it seems clear that decreasing appetite works to fight infection by saving energy and allowing the body to focus on healing. Conserving energy is important in the healing of any illness, and decreasing appetite works to fight infection by saving energy and allowing the body to focus its resources on healing.

2. Not eating cuts off the body's supply of nutrients, meaning it also keeps the infection from feeding off the nutrients it needs to spread. Infections especially feed on iron and zinc in order to grow.

3. Not eating pushes the body to eliminate infection cells through the process of cell apoptosis.

The type of infection you are suffering from may determine whether eating or fasting is beneficial to healing. Studies suggest that fasting may be best to fight bacterial infections, and eating may be best for fighting viruses. Experiments on mice with bacterial infections showed that those which were force-fed had a lower survival rate than mice that were left to eat based on their own hunger. Overall, evidence indicates that fasting is primarily helpful in the early stages of a bacterial infection. Your best bet is to follow your body's natural cues and eat when you are hungry rather than forcing yourself to eat, as this may worsen your condition.

Health

Intermittent fasting has been linked to protection against various diseases. There is also evidence indicating that practicing intermittent fasting can lengthen your lifespan. It is possible that intermittent fasting helps prevent cancer, Alzheimer's disease, heart disease, type 2 diabetes, and more.

1. Cancer: fasting for short periods could help cancer patients prevent damage from chemotherapy and increase the effectiveness of treatment overall.

   Alzheimer's disease: fasting is proven to boost brain health. In particular, fasting helpsprevent neurodegenerative diseases like Alzheimer's, Huntington's, and Parkinson's disease.

2. Heart disease: intermittent fasting in particular can help reduce the risk of heart disease by reducing different factors that can cause heart disease. Fasting reduces overall weight, cholesterol, and blood pressure. Lowering these factors helps the body become less susceptible to heart disease.

3. Type 2 diabetes: intermittent fasting could help regulate blood sugar levels by lowering levels of the hormone insulin in the body. This may also have positive effects on those with insulin resistance.

4. Oxidative stress: oxidative stress refers to a disturbance in the balance of free radicals (also known as reactive oxygen species) and the body's antioxidant defenses. Intermittent fasting can help prevent all diseases in general by lowering oxidative stress and decreasing inflammation.

Note that the benefits of fasting that produce the positive effects on the diseases listed above could possibly be solely a result of weight loss (which is a result of fasting), instead of from the fasting itself. Regardless, either fasting or the results of fasting has a proven effective in reducing the risk of many illnesses and diseases.

Save time

Some people implement intermittent fasting in order to simply and streamline an aspect of their lives. Meal planning and preparation can take up a lot of time and energy. Having a set plan for when you will eat each meal and eating fewer snacks and calories saves a lot of time and brain space.

Save money

Just as intermittent fasting works to save time, eating less frequently and fewer calories means saving money on groceries and meals out. If you are following your fasting plan of choice, you may find that happy hour drinks simply do not fit into your fast. This doesn't mean that you are forced to forego all meals out or social occasions with food and drink. It just means that you might not be able to partake if the time does not fit into your fast. You can also try to schedule these outings within the limits of your fast.

How Does Intermittent Fasting Work?

There are various methods of fasting, but what they all have in common is a predetermined period of not eating cycled with predetermined periods for meals and snacks. As long as you are making healthy choices in the foods you eat during your preplanned eating time, you can expect to see a variety of health benefits from intermittent fasting. It is an effective way to limit your calorie intake, improve your metabolic health, and burn fat. You may also experience effects on your mental health as a result of simplifying eating habits. The time and money you save can help reduce stress and ease anxiety. Depending on the time you choose to start fasting, you may experience better sleep at night.

When most people think of diet plans, they think it is going to mean giving up certain kinds of foods or eating less than they want to feel satisfied. But with intermittent fasting, you do not necessarily have to sacrifice eating the foods you want, in the amounts you want. The only guidelines fasting gives is the timing of your meals. However, depending on your goals for fasting, you may want to alter your other dietary habits as well. It is important to eat vitamin-rich, nutritious foods while intermittent fasting to stay healthy and satisfied during the period of not eating.

Burn Fat

Many dieters find intermittent fasting to be a practical and relatively easy way to lose fat. Research shows that intermittent fasting is at least as effective of a method as cutting calories to lose weight, if not even more so. Studies have proven intermittent fasting can help you lose 3-8% of your body weight in just1-6 months. In fact, intermittent fasting may be a more effective, safer, and healthier approach to weight loss in obese people than counting calories.

Intermittent fasting works to burn fat by boosting the metabolism and improving overall metabolic health. It does this through affecting several hormones, which are chemicals that control many important processes in the body, including the metabolism. Hormones are connected to appetite and cravings, how muchyou eat, and how much fat youburn or store in your body. Intermittent fasting works for weight loss by improving the balance of several hormones that help the body burn fat.

Insulin

You may have heard of the hormone insulin in the context of treating diabetes. Too much insulin is linked to type 2 diabetes, heart disease, cancer, and obesity. It is an important hormone for proper fat metabolism. Insulin is responsible for telling the body when to stop breaking down fat and store it. Intermittent fasting is as effective as cutting calories for lowering your body's insulin levels. Research shows that It is possible that through intermittent fasting alone you could decrease insulin levels by as much as 20-31%.

Human Growth Hormone

Human growth hormone is another chemical that is important when talking about burning fat. While you want to reduce insulin levels to lose weight, you want to increase human growth hormone. This is because higher amounts of human growth hormone in the blood is linked to greater fat loss. Not only can higher levels of human growth hormone improve fat burning, it can also help preserve muscle mass.

It is important to note that women might not experience as much of an increase in human growth hormone as men while fasting. But during studies, men showed an increase of human growth hormone levels by as much as five times.

Norepinephrine

You may have heard of the hormone norepinephrine in the context of treating anxiety and depression. Norepinephrine is typically more associated with stress than fat burning, although it affects both.

Norepinephrine is the hormone that causes the "fight or flight" reaction to distressing situations in humans and other animals. You know that feeling when you are in a confrontation with someone, and you have an almost animalistic urge to either run away or punch the other person? That's norepinephrine working in your body. It helps animals react to predators and other dangers, and back in cave-dwelling days, it used to help defend humans against predators, too. Now that humans do not have the same threats as then, we get this same "fight or flight" response from other triggers, such as stress from work and relationships. We also get a surge of the "fight or flight" feeling when we are in immediate danger, like when we experience a car accident. Norepinephrine increases attention and alertness to react better in these situations.

Not only does norepinephrine activate the "fight or flight" response, it also tells fat cells in the body to release fatty acids. An increase in norepinephrine means the body can burn more fat. Intermittent fasting helps increase the levels of norepinephrine in the bloodstream.

Boost Metabolism

You may be wondering how intermittent fasting can work to boost the metabolism, when we have been told that skipping meals will make your body compensate for the lack of incoming calories by storing more fat and slowing its metabolism.

It is true that fasting for too long of periods of time causes a decrease in metabolism. However, strategically fasting for short periods of time can actually increase the metabolism rather than slowing it down. Short-term fasting can increase metabolism by as much as 14%. This is most likely connected to the rise in norepinephrine, the "fight or flight" hormone, in the bloodstream. So intermittent fasting is proven to boost metabolism but fasting for too long can have the opposite effect.

If you are still worried about fasting slowing down your metabolism, you should note that intermittent fasting decreases metabolism less than a long period of cutting calories.

Your metabolism naturally slows down as you lose weight. This is partially because weight loss causes muscles loss, and muscle tissue is always burning calories. Loss of muscle mass is not the only reason why the metabolism slows down from weight loss, though.

Your body has a natural defense mechanism against starvation. If your body is not getting enough calories to survive it automatically goes into starvation mode, officially known as "adaptive thermogenesis." Calories are energy, and your body slows the metabolism to conserve energy if it thinks there are no more calories coming in.

This is illustrated by the participants of the well-known reality television showed called The Biggest Loser. Overweight/obese participants are challenged through a program, of diet and exercise to lose large amounts of weight quickly. This entails a strict low-calorie diet and a high level of intense workouts among people who are not used to restricting their calorie intake and exercising.

Although participants lose large amounts of weight during filming, a few years later almost all of them regained nearly all the weight back that they lost on the show. Worse still, their metabolic rates had gone down during filming because of the body's starvation mode, and never went back up. This means it actually became harder for them to lose or even maintain their weight after dropping a large number of pounds quickly on the program.

This applies not only to participants on The Biggest Loser, but for anyone who seeks a quick fix for weight loss through restricting calories and an intense exercise regime. Research has proven that rapid weight loss through these means can ultimately slow down metabolism, making it nearly impossible to maintain the weight loss.

Because intermittent fasting only causes short-term effects on the hormones that promote fat burning, it is likely that using intermittent fasting as a dietary aid will not have the same problem of reducing metabolic rate like long-term calorie restriction. Studies have proven that alternate-day fasting did not cause a decrease in metabolism rate over a three-week period. Note that there is no current research on whether or not long-term intermittent fasting decreases metabolic rate.

Retain muscle mass

Muscles are composed of metabolically active tissue, which means that having more muscle mass keeps your metabolic rate higher. With greater muscle mass, you burn more calories, even while resting. However, fat loss during weight loss is usually accompanied by muscle loss. It is possible that intermittent fasting preserves more muscle mass than cutting calories.

This is primarily due to the boost in hormones that burn fat caused by intermittent fasting. Intermittent fasting increases levels of human growth hormone in the bloodstream, which helps to retain muscle mass even during weight loss. Like its long-term effects on metabolism, there needs to be more conclusive research conducted on intermittent fasting's effects on muscle mass.

The Different Fasting Methods

There are many methods of fasting, and you may want to experiment with several variations before you find the way that works best for your body and schedule. Different fasting methods involve cutting out different foods and drinks for different periods of time. Below are some of the most well-known methods of fasting.

Absolute fasting

Absolute fasting requires you not to eat or drink anything at all, not even water. Absolute fasting should only be practiced for short periods of time. Indeed, it would be impossible to survive more than a few days without water or any other sustenance.

Water fasting

Water fasting is similar to absolute fasting, with the exception being that water is permitted. You can go much longer on a water fast than an absolute fast, because the body can survive on water alone for up to a month.

Juice fasting

Juice cleansing has become an increasingly popular diet and health trend in recent years. It is also referred to as juice detoxing or juice cleansing. Juice fasting usually involves exclusively drinking fruit and vegetable juices, and water. Juice fasting typically does not including eating whole fruits and vegetables. Blended drinks like smoothies may or may not be allowed on a juice cleanse.

Intermittent fasting

Intermittent fasting involves cycling predetermined periods of eating and periods of fasting. The fasting period of an intermittent fast can last as long as 24 hours. This is different from an absolute fast, which does not include a period of eating.

The 16:8 Method

The 16:8 methodis one of the most popular ways of practicing an intermittent fast. Many claim it is an easy and convenient way to maintain and lose weight in a healthy way. Unlike calorie restriction or an intense exercise program, the 16:8 method of fasting is great for burning fat and seeing results with minimal effort. It is believed that this method of weight loss is more sustainable than others and will make participants less likely to regain weight than traditional calorie counting and exercise.

How does the 16:8 Method work?

To implement the 16:8 method of fasting, you must limit your food and beverage intake by only consuming during an 8-hour period of each day and abstaining from food for the remaining 16 hours. During the 16-hour period of fasting, you are typically allowed to drink as much water and low or no calorie beverages, such as coffee and tea. You can practice this fast as often as you would like, from just one day a week to a daily habit. It depends on what your goals are and your individual health needs.

Many find this dietary plan easier to follow than other diets because instead of counting calories, eliminating certain foods from your diet, or implementing a new workout routine, all you have to do for the 16:8 method is pay attention to when you are eating. It easily fits into most lifestyles and is good for people who have trouble sticking to a diet plan or fitness routine. It can be practiced anywhere by anyone.

Where do I have to pay special attention?

Like any dietary plan, it is best to talk to your doctor before starting the 16:8 method to make sure it is a safe option for you. Certain health conditions that require frequent eating, such as type 1 diabetes, may preclude you from participating in the 16:8 method. Intermittent fasting has different effects on women and men, so women especially who are pregnant, breast-feeding, or trying to become pregnant are strongly advised to discuss the 16:8 fasting method with their doctors before trying the dietary plan. If you have a history of easting disorders, please talk to a doctor before trying the 16:8 method.

Choose the 8-hour window in which you plan to eat carefully. Many who practice the 16:8 method of intermittent fasting choose 11:00 a.m. to 7:00 p.m., or 12:00 p.m. to 8:00 p.m. This means they are effectively fasting through breakfast or eating it very late/combining it with lunch and are not snacking late into the evening or eating late at night, a dietary pitfall many experience. You may select any 8-hour window; this should not change the efficacy of the 16:8 method. Be sure to choose time where you will feel full and sustained through any work, fitness routine, classes, etc. that you do on a typical day.

Be sure to fill up on nutrient-rich foods to keep your energy up during the hours of fasting. Although intermittent fasting doesn't technically require you to change the foods you eat or your portion sizes, making healthy choices and watching your portion sizes will help you have more success sticking to the 16:8 method, help you feel better while fasting, and ultimately help you meet whatever your goals are for fasting.

Pay attention to how much you are eating during your 8-hour window. Some participants may find that they eat more than usual during the 8-hour window, either intentionally because they think they need to cram in as many calories as possible to sustain themselves through the fast, or unintentionally because they have increased hunger. Keeping track of your portion sizes and the nutritional value of the foods you are eating will help stave off hunger and prevent you from overeating.

Most people drink water and other low or no calorie beverages during the 16-hour fast period. Be sure not to choose high calorie smoothies or sugary drinks during the fasting period, as this goes against the rules of the fast and you will not experience the same benefits. There are many healthy and low-calorie beverages you can enjoy to stay hydrated and satisfied during the fasting period.

Tips

Don't be put off by the sound of going 16 hours without eating! Odds are that you are already fasting for about half of those 16 hours naturally by sleeping.

Some people start practicing the 16:8 method on the weekend or vacation so that they can give the dietary plan their full attention, while others may elect to start when they are very busy to keep their mind preoccupied and not focused on any hunger they may experience. Remember, you decide how often you want to practice this method of fasting, and you can experiment with which days to fast depending on what feels best to you.

Conclusion

The 16:8 method of fasting can be an easy and sustainable way to maintain or lose weight and increase overall health. Talk to your doctor first before starting this or any other dietary plan to make sure it is right for you.

The 5:2 Method

How does the 5:2 method work?

The 5:2 method of intermittent fasting is a variation of the 16:8 method. Instead of restricting eating to a window of 8 hours per day, the 5:2 method works by reducing calorie consumption to 25% of your recommended daily caloric intake for 2 days of the week and eating your normal number of calories for the remaining 5 days. You can choose which days to fast, and they do not need to be consecutive nor on the same days of the week each week. In fact, it is advised not to schedule your fasting days consecutively, as this increases the likelihood of breaking your fast or not meet your body's nutritional needs.

For example, the standard rule of thumb for caloric intake is that adults need 2,000 calories per day. This may vary based on weight, activity level, age, gender, and more. If your recommended caloric intake is 2,000 per day, then 25% of 2,000 is 500 calories. That means 2 days a week you must reduce your calories to 500 and maintain 2,000 calories the remaining 5 days.

Where do I have to pay special attention?

Unlike the 16:8 method, with the 5:2 method there are no restrictions on the timing of when you eat your meals during fasting days. You just need to keep your total caloric intake at 25% of your typical dietary needs. Although the standard recommended caloric intake for adults is around 2,000 calories, make sure you talk with your doctor to determine the correct number of calories you should be consuming daily.

Be sure that you aren't "cheating" this method, intentionally or unintentionally. Some make the mistake of overeating on the days of not fasting, either on purpose thinking it will make the fasting days easier, or because they are hungry. Although there are no restrictions regarding the timing of meals for this method of fasting, you will want to experiment with the timing of your meals so that you stay full through your fasting days without exceeding your recommended caloric intake on your regular eating days.

You must be careful not to exceed your recommended daily intake on normal eating days to make the 5:2 method work for you. Some make the mistake of carefully counting their calories on fasting days, only to eat over their standard recommended daily calories on normal eating days and therefore rendering the fast less effective. The 5:2 method requires you to keep track of your caloric intake not only on your 2 days of fasting, but on the remaining 5 days of normal eating as well.

Tips

Eating several small meals throughout the day (while staying within the guidelines of 25% of your total recommended caloric intake) during fasting days will help keep your energy up, stay feeling full, and balance your blood sugar levels. You could also try just one large meal accompanied by snacks throughout the day. Preferences will vary; you will want to experiment and find what works best for you.

Unlike the 16:8 diet, fasting on the 5:2 does not require you to limit your beverages to water and other zero or low-calorie drinks. In fact, smoothies and juices are a great way to stay full and consume the necessary nutrients on fasting days. Just be sure you aren't having tons of sugary or super high-calorie drinks, as this can quickly take up your total caloric allotment for fasting days, and a sugar crash can make you feel lethargic and hungry later on.

Conclusion

The 5:2 method may be right for you if you want to try an intermittent fasting dietary plan but would prefer to cut calories 2 days a week and eat how you normally do on the other days instead of eating only 8 hours out of the day, like you would on the 16:8 method. Make sure you are sticking to 25% of your total recommended daily caloric intake on fasting days and eating healthy foods to sustain your energy. Find out the correct recommended caloric intake for you personally based on various factors so that you can best calculate your calorie allotment for fasting days (and non-fasting days, too!).

30 Day Weight-Loss Plan

No matter which method of intermittent fasting you decide is best for you and want to try, it is important to eat nutritious and low-calorie meals to have the best results and make the fasting process easier.

Goal Setting

To get the best results you must first determine what your ideal results would be. Doyou want to shed a specific number of pounds by a particular date? Are you seeking to lower your cholesterol or balance your blood sugar levels? Do you want to lose a certain number of inches off your waistline or thighs?

Having a goal set in mind will help keep you on track during your fast. Try not to set unreachable goals or have unreasonably high expectations form your fast. Remember, intermittent fasting is meant to be a lifestyle, not a fad diet or fast-track to weight loss. Choosing the fasting method that works best for you can be an easy and sustainable way to meet your goals without reverting back to your original weight.

Talk to your doctor or a nutritionist about how much weight/inches/etc. you can reasonably expect to lose if you follow your chosen method of intermittent fasting.

30 Day Weight-Loss Plan

The following recipes are particularly helpful for the 5:2 method, as the caloric content of each recipe should be below almost every person's 25% of standard caloric intake. That means all of these recipes should be allowed during the 2 days of fasting on the 5:2 plan.

These recipes also work for the 16:8 method because they are nutritious and filling and can help you stay full and satisfied during the fasting period of your day.

Before starting your 30-day weight loss plan, talk to your doctor or nutritionist about how much weight you can reasonably expect to lose form your chosen method in a 30-day period. Some see results around 15 pounds after 20 days of intermittent fasting, while some experience a 1 or 2 pound loss per week. There are many variables (level of fitness and activity, starting weight, age and gender, etc.) that will affect how much weight you may expect to lose after 30 days of intermittent fasting. Make sure you set a reasonable goal and remind yourself that intermittent fasting is meant to be a minimal effort lifestyle change for losing weight and improving your overall health.

Using the following recipes can help you reach your goals during your 30 days of whichever fasting method you choose. The calories for each recipe are listed to help you keep track if you are doing the 5:2 method, and all of the dishes are nutritious options for staying full if you are doing the 16:8 method.

Banana Yogurt Crunch

Preparation time: 5 minutes

No cooking required

Servings: 2

Vegetarian

Yogurt and banana combine to make the perfect low-calorie breakfast that keeps you full and satisfied until lunchtime. This recipe can be used for breakfast, or for a snack any time of day. The banana adds a natural sweetness without the need for added sugars, and the seeds or nuts give the dish a satisfying crunch.

As part of anintermittent fastingdiet plan, 1 servingof banana yogurt crunch provides: 2-3of your dailydairy portions and your daily piece of fruit. This meal is about 150 calories preserving.

Ingredients

- 12 oz fat-free Greek yogurt

- 1 banana, peeled and sliced

- ½ ounce mixed seeds (sunflower, pumpkin, sesame), and/or nuts (almonds, walnuts)

Preparation

1. Divide the Greek yogurt into two portions in separate bowls. Arrange the banana slices on top. Sprinkle with seeds and/or nuts and serve.

TIP:

When grocery shopping, be on the lookout for bags of premixed seeds and containers of mixed nuts. These can be used and add variety to a number of meals on the intermittent fasting dietary plan. Make sure they do not have added salts and sugars, as this can add to your calorie count.

Bacon and Tomato Poached Eggs

Preparation time: less than 20 minutes

Cooking time: less than 15 minutes

Servings: 2

Instead of a traditional English breakfast or a meal heavy in fried foods, try this flavorful, low-calorie breakfast. You could even have it for a fun breakfast for dinner option! Poached eggs are a greatway to reduce the number of calories in an egg dish and are surprisingly easy to make.

As part of an intermittent fasting diet plan, 1 serving of bacon and tomato poached eggs provides 1 out of 6 of your recommended daily portions of vegetables, and your one daily salty food. It is also high in protein thanks to the bacon and eggs. This meal provides 210 calories per serving.

Ingredients

- ◆ 2 cage-free eggs

- ◆ 2 ripe tomatoes, cut in halves

- ◆ 4 strips of low-fat, low-sodium bacon

- ◆ Black pepper

- ◆ Sea salt

Preparation

1. Preheat your grill to the highest setting. While the grill is preheating, line a grill pan with foil and set the halved tomatoes on it. Grind black pepper over tomatoes to taste.

2. Allow the tomatoes to grill for about 3 minutes. Without yet removing the tomatoes, add the uncooked bacon slices to the grill and continue to grill with the tomatoes for an additional 4 minutes, making sure to flip the bacon after two minutes to cook evenly. The bacon should be lightly browned on each side.

3. Halfway fill a medium saucepan with water andbring to boil. Crack eggs into two small separate bowls, making sure to keep the yolks intact. Reduce the heat until the water simmers gently. Carefully slidethe eggs into the simmering water and allow to cook for about 3 minutes, or until the whites are set but the yolks arerunny.

4. Use a spoon (not a spatula, as you may break the yolks) to scoop the poached eggs out of the pan and place one on two separate serving plates. Arrange the cooked tomatoes and bacon on the plate. Add black pepper and salt to taste and serve immediatelywhile still hot.

Tropical Green Smoothie

Preparation time: less than 10 minutes

No cooking required

Servings: 1

Vegetarian

This delightful smoothie will make you feel like you're vacationing by the ocean and is packed full of vitamins and nutrients. If it weren't for the green color, you wouldn't even know it has spinach in it! This recipe requires a food processor or blender. You can use fresh or frozen fruit, but frozen fruit will save you money, store well, and naturally chill the smoothie without adding ice. This smoothie is great for a breakfast replacement option, or for a filling and sweet snack.

As part of an intermittent fasting diet plan, 1 serving of tropical green smoothie provides: 1/3 (2 out of 6) of your recommended daily portions of vegetables, and your daily piece of fruit. This recipe provides about 300 calories per serving.

Ingredients

- ½ cup spinach

- ½ cup fresh orange juice (not form concentrate)

- ½ banana

- ¼ cup frozen or fresh mango chunks

- ¼ cup frozen or fresh pineapple chunks

- 1 tbsp shredded coconut, plus a pinch for sprinkling

- 1 tsp honey or agave nectar (optional)

- 1 tsp hemp or other seeds (optional)

Preparation

1. Blend all ingredients in blender or food processor until all ingredients are fully mixed and the smoothie is the correct consistency. If you use fresh fruit instead of frozen, add one or two ice cubes for temperature and texture and process again. The liquid should be thick and rich but still pour easily from the blender. You can adjust the amount of juice to change the consistency.

2. Pour into a tall glass, sprinkle with extra shredded coconut and serve with a straw.

3. Tips: For extra nutritional value, add a tablespoon of collagen protein powder and/ or a teaspoon of spirulina powder. This recipe is great for adjusting to get different flavors! Try substituting the pineapple and mango for berries or substitute the orange juice with almond milk and a spoonful of Greek yogurt. The possibilities are endless!

Mushroom and Garlic Frittata

Preparation time: less than 20 minutes

Cooking time: less than 20 minutes

Servings: 2

Vegetarian

Mushrooms and garlic bring delightful flavoring to this easy to make and low-calorie frittata. This dish is great for breakfast, or for a fun breakfast for dinner option. You could also serve with a side salad for lunch.

As part of an intermittent fasting dietary plan, 1 serving of mushroom and garlic frittata provides half (3 out of 6) of your daily recommended portions of vegetables. It is also high in protein from the eggs, and high in antioxidants from the garlic. This meal contains 245 calories, 14 grams of protein, 3.5 grams of carbs, and 14 grams of fat.

Ingredients

- ◆ Cooking spray

- ◆ 9 oz sliced chestnut mushrooms

- ◆ 1 crushed clove of garlic

- ◆ 1 tbsp thinly sliced chives

- ◆ 4 beaten cage-free eggs

- ◆ Black pepper

For optional side salad:

- ◆ 1 Little Gemlettuce, with the leaves separated

- ◆ 3.5 oz cherry tomatoes, cut in halves

- ◆ 1/3 cucumber,cut into chunksor cubes

- ◆ Ground sea salt

- ◆ Ground black pepper

- ◆ Olive oil (optional)

Preparation

1. Prepare a small frying pan (no wider than about 7 inches at its base) by spraying with cooking oil and place over high heat. Stir-fry the mushrooms (you may need to do cook the mushrooms in batches in the small pan) for 2-3 minutes or until they are lightly browned and softened. Strain the cooked mushrooms of any juices to keep the mushrooms from getting soggy, then return them to the frying pan. Add the crushed garlic and sliced chivesand sprinkle with the ground black pepper. Cook for one more minute on the high setting, thenreduce heat tolow.

2. Preheat your grill to the hottest setting. Pour the beaten eggs over the mushroom/garlic/chive mix in the pan. Cook the frittata for 5 minutes or until the eggs are almost set. Move the pan to the grill for 3-4 minutes, or until the eggs are fully set. If you are serving with the optional side salad, combine all salad ingredients into a bowl and toss. Add seasonings and/or olive oil to taste.

3. Take the frittata pan off the grill and loosen the sides of the dish with a knife. Place on a dish or board and cut into triangular slices. This frittata can be served cold or hot with optional side salad.

TIP:

Use a non-stick frying pan to make the removal of the frittata easier. Be sure to use a small size pan to achieve the desired thickness.

Italian Omelet

Preparation time: less than 30 minutes

Cooking time: less than 10 minutes

Servings: 1

Omelets aren't just for breakfast! This hearty Italian omelet makes a filling meal for any time of day. Think of it as an Italian sub sandwich but substitute the bread for high protein and low carb eggs instead! This easy to whip up omelet combines the salty flavors of prosciutto with creamy mozzarella and tomatoes and basil for a satisfying meal. You can even serve it with a simple side salad for an extra serving of vegetables.

As part of an intermittent fasting diet plan, 1 whole Italian omelet provides 1/3 (2 out of 6) of your daily vegetable portions, and your 1 daily serving of dairy. It is high in protein from the egg, prosciutto, and mozzarella. This meal provides 450 calories, 35 grams of protein, 3.5 grams of carbohydrates, and 39 grams of fat.

Ingredients

- 2 tbsp extra virgin olive oil, separated
- 6-8 cherry or grape tomatoes

- ♦ 1 tbsp chopped fresh basil
- ♦ 2 slices prosciutto
- ♦ Slices of fresh mozzarella, to taste
- ♦ 3 cage-free eggs
- ♦ Sea salt
- ♦ Black pepper

Preparation

1. Heat 1 tablespoon of the extra virgin olive oil in a small frying pan and on medium heat. While the oil is warming, cut the tomatoes into quarters and chop the prosciutto and mozzarella into small chunks.

2. Crack the eggs into a small bowl and beat with awhisk until they are frothy.Season with salt and pepper, then pour directly into the warm pan. Allow to cook for 1 minute, then use a spatula to gently lift the underside of the egg to make sure it won't stick.

3. Cook the eggs until the top looks almost set at the center. Sprinkle the mozzarella, prosciutto, basil, and tomatoes over one side of omelet.

4. Using a spatula, fold the empty half of the omelet over to envelop the fillings. Turn off the stove but leave the pan to sit on the burner for an additional minute. Drizzle the remaining tablespoon of olive oil over the omelet and season with more salt and pepper to taste.

5. Use a spatula to gently slide the omelet onto a plate and serve immediately.

TIP:

Remember, prosciutto is very salty, so start small when adding salt, or leave it out entirely. To make this a vegetarian dish, you can leave out the prosciutto.

Cinnamon Pear Porridge

Preparation time: less than 30 minutes

Cooking time: less than 10 minutes

Servings: 2

Vegetarian

This delicious porridge is low-calorie since it is prepared with water and skimmed milk. Cinnamon provides a sweetener without adding any sugars, and the juicy grated pear contributes to the flavor and texture.

As part of an intermittent fasting diet plan, 1 serving of cinnamon pear porridge provides ½ (3 out of 6) of your daily recommended portions of vegetables, and 1 of your dairy portions. Each serving contains about 220 calories.

Ingredients

- ◆ 2.5 oz oats
- ◆ ¼ tsp ground cinnamon, plus some extra for sprinkling
- ◆ 10 oz semi-skimmed milk
- ◆ 1 ripened pear
- ◆ 1 lemon wedge

Preparation

1. Combine the cinnamon, oats, and milk in a non-stick saucepan cook over low tomedium heat forabout 4-5 minutes. Stir consistently until the consistency is creamy and rich. Pour or ladle into two bowls.

2. Grate the pear and arrangeon top of thehot porridge. Squeeze the lemon wedge over the pear and sprinkle with the extra ground cinnamon. Serve hot.

TIP:

Be sure to use whole or jumbo oats instead of instant or ground oats, since they take longer to digest and will help keep you full longer during intermittent fasting.

Yogurt with Berries

Preparation time: less than 30 minutes

No cooking required

Servings: 2

Vegetarian

This delicious, fruity yogurt makes a tasty and filling breakfast or snack. You can use frozen or fresh berries but using frozen berries will help you save money and the juices add sweetness and flavor as the berries thaw.

As part of an intermittent fasting diet plan, 1 serving of berry yogurt provides your daily allowed piece of fruit, and 2 of your daily servings of dairy. This dish contains 150 calories per serving.

Ingredients

♦ 6 oz fresh or frozen (and defrosted) mixed berries, or the berry of your choice

♦ 12 oz fat-free Greek yogurt

♦ 10 oz toasted almond flakes or almond slivers

Preparation

1. Spoon half of the yogurt into two small bowls or glasses. Top with half of the berries. Layer the remaining yogurt on top of the berries, and the rest of the berries on top of the second yogurt layer.

2. Sprinkle the toasted almond flakes or slivered almonds on top and serve.

TIPS:

There are lots of ways to change up this recipe! It also stores well and the juices from the berries make the yogurt even more flavorful if you store this dish in the fridge. You can swap out the almonds for walnuts, pumpkin seeds, hemp seeds, or any nut or seed for a crunch (note that this will affect the number of calories). For some additional sweetness, you can sprinkle raw sugar or drizzle honey over the berries, although this will add sugar and calories.

Mushroom Delight

Preparation time: less than 30 minutes

Cooking time: less than 30 minutes

Servings: 1

Mushrooms in any dish during intermittent fasting are a great choice because they are nutritious and very low in calories. This dish is great for any time of day, but especially for breakfast or brunch.

As part of an intermittent fasting diet plan, 1 serving of mushroom delight provides 1 of your 3 daily servings of dairy, and 1/3 (2 out of 6) of your daily servings of vegetables. There is also plenty of protein from the eggs and antioxidants from the garlic. This dish contains 270 calories per serving.

Ingredients

- 10 oz chopped Portobello mushrooms
- 3 oz chopped green beans
- 2 oz grated zucchini
- 1 spring onion
- 2 cage-free eggs
- 1 minced clove of garlic
- .5 oz w mustard
- .5 oz grated cheese

Preparation

1. Combine all ingredients except the eggs and grated cheese in a non-stick frying pan. No cooking oil is needed as the mushrooms will release water while cooking. Cook for 5-10 minutes over high heat.

2. Break the eggs over the mixture. Allow to cook for an additional 2 minutes, or until the egg whites are firm. Yolks can be runny or cook for another minute to firm yolks.

3. Remove the frying pan from heat. Scoop mushroom delightonto a plate orinto a bowl.Sprinkle with the grated cheese and serve hot.

Baked Moroccan Eggs

Preparation time: less than 30 minutes

Cooking time: less than 3 minutes

Servings: 2

Vegetarian

These baked Moroccan eggs make the perfect dish for brunch and baking the eggs instead of frying them saves calories. This dish pairs well with a small side salad, such as the one described in the recipe for the mushroom and garlic frittata.

As part of an intermittent fasting diet plan, 1 serving of baked Moroccan eggs provides 1/3 (2 out of 6) of your recommended daily servings of vegetables. This meal contains 170 calories per serving.

Ingredients

- ½ tbsp cooking oil
- ½ chopped onion
- 1 sliced clove of garlic

- ½ tsp ras-el-hanout (can substitutewith a mixture of equal partscoriander, ginger, and paprika, OR just coriander)

- Ground cinnamon (pinch)

- ½ tsp ground coriander

- 14 oz chopped cherry tomatoes

- 2 tbsp choppedcoriander

- 2 cage-free eggs

- Sea

- Black pepper

Preparation

1. Preheat your oven to 400 degrees Fahrenheit. Coat a frying pan with cooking oil. Add the sliced garlic and the chopped onions and cook for about 5 minutes or until soft, but not soggy. Add all the spices (including only the ground coriander, not the chopped coriander) and stir over heat for another minute.

2. Add the chopped cherry tomatoes and season with ground salt and pepper. Simmeron low heat for another 8-10 minutes.

3. Sprinkle half (1 tbsp) of the chopped coriander over the dish. Separate the vegetable and spices mixture evenly between two small oven-safe dishes. Break an egg over each dish.

4. Place the two dishes in the oven and cook for 8-10 minutes, or untilthe egg whites are firm but the yolks are still runny. You may cook for an additional 2-3 minutesif you prefer theyolks to be solid.

5. Sprinkle the remaining tablespoon of chopped coriander over the dishes and serve warm.

TIP:

If you would like this dish to be a little spicy, add some chili powder to taste. Start with just a pinch and work your way so as not to make it too spicy. As part of an intermittent fasting diet, you may want to pair this dish with a glass of skimmed milk (70 calories) to add a portion of dairy and increase fullness until your next meal.

Hot Chicken Salad

Preparation time: less than 30 minutes

Cooking time: less than 30 minutes

Servings: 2

This salad is a healthy, low-fat take on traditional chicken salad that you can serve either hot or cold. This dish is perfect for lunch, dinner, or even as a hearty side salad.

As part of an intermittent fasting diet plan, 1 serving of hot chicken salad provides 1/3 (2 out of 6) of your recommended daily vegetable portions. This dish contains 200 calories per serving.

Ingredients

- 2 boned and skinned chicken breasts, cut into halves

- Cooking spray

- 1 red or orangepepper, cut intochunks with seeds removed

- 1 head of little gem lettuce with the leaves separated

- 2 oz watercress (remove tough stalks)

- 2 tomatoes cut into chunks

- ⅓ sliced cucumber

- 1 tsp balsamic vinegar

- ½ lemon

- Sea salt

- Black pepper

Preparation

1. Season each piece of chicken on each side with salt and pepper. Coat a large non-stick frying pan with cooking oil or spray and place on high heat. Cook the seasoned chicken pieces in the pan for about 3 minutes on each side or until slightly browned and cooked through. Remove cooked chickenfrom pan and set on a plate.

2. Spray the frying pan again with cooking oil and fry the chunks of red or orange pepper for 3 minutes on each side or until slightly soft,but not mushy.

3. Divide the watercress, lettuce leaves, tomato chunks, cucumber slices and cooked peppers between two plates. Slice the cooked chicken breast halves and arrange on top of salads. Dress salad with balsamic vinegarand squeeze the juice of the lemon half over both dishes. Season with salt and pepper and serve.

TIP:

If you prefer a cold salad, you can allow the cooked peppers and chicken to chill in the refrigerator or at room temperature before adding them to the salad greens. You can also leave the peppers uncooked for a cold dish and firmer texture.

Cozy Vegetable Soup

Preparation time: less than 30 minutes

Cooking time:30 minutes to 1 hour

Servings: 2

Vegetarian

This hearty soup is full of nutrients and flavor and is perfect to curl up on a couch with on cold night. You can serve this soup for dinner, or pack in a thermos as a convenient hot lunch on the go. You can even use a small portion as a healthy side dish to complete and add nutrition to a larger meal.

As part of an intermittent diet plan, 1 serving of cozy vegetable soup provides your 1 allowed daily salty food, and 3 out of 5 of your recommended daily recommended vegetable portions. This dish contains 220 calories per serving.

Ingredients

- Cooking spray
- 1 sliced onion
- 2 sliced cloves of garlic
- 2 sliced celery sticks

- 2carrots cut intochunks
- 14 oz canned tomato chunks
- 1 cube vegetable stock
- 1 tsp mixed herbs/ seasonings
- 14 oz canned limabeans, rinsed and drained
- 4 oz (1 head) sliced spring greens
- Sea salt
- Black pepper

Preparation

1. Coat a saucepan with cooking oil and combine the garlic, onion, celery and carrots over medium heatfor about 10 minutes. Stir until soft but not mushy.

2. Add the chopped tomatoes and 26 oz of water the pan. Crumble the cube of stock into the pan and stir inalong with the herbs or seasonings. Increase the heat to a boil, then reduce heat to a simmer and allowto cook for another 20 minutes.

3. Add in the lima beans and spring greens. Continue to simmer on low heat for an additional 3-4 minutes until the greens are soft. Season soup with ground salt and pepper to taste. Ladle into two bowls and serve hot.

TIP:

This is a great recipe to double or even triple if you want to store and eat over a few days. The lima beans can be substituted with another varieties of beans, such as cannellini, if preferred.

Roasted Vegetables with Chermoula Tofu

Preparation time: less than 30 minutes

Cooking time: 30 minutes to 1 hour

Servings: 4

Vegetarian

Tofu is great for absorbing the flavors of the chermoula in this meal. Serve with roasted vegetables for a healthy and hearty vegetarian dish great for any time of the year. This meal is a perfect option for lunch or dinner.

As part of an intermittent fasting diet plan, 1 serving of roasted vegetables with chermoula tofu provides 1/3 (2 out of 6) of your recommended daily vegetable portions. This meal contains 180 calories per serving.

Ingredients

For chermoula tofu:

- 1 oz chopped coriander
- 3 chopped cloves of garlic
- 1 tsp crushed cumin seeds
- Grated rind of 1 lemon
- ½ tsp crushed dried chilies
- 1 tbsp olive oil
- 9 oz tofu

For roasted vegetables:

- 2 quartered red onions
- 2 sliced zucchinis
- 2 sliced red peppers with seeds removed
- 2 sliced yellow peppers with seeds rcmoved
- 1 sliced eggplant
- Cooking spray
- Sea salt

Preparation

1. Preheat the oven to 400 degreesFahrenheit. Forthe chermoula, combine thecoriander, garlic, cumin seeds, lemon rind, dried chilies, oil,and a pinch of salt in a bowl. Blot the tofu dry with paper towels and cut in half, then cut each of the halves into thin horizontal slices. Spread the chermoula thickly over the sliced tofu.

2. Arrange all the vegetables in an oven-safe pan and coat with cooking spray oil. Bake vegetables on their own in theoven for about 45 minutes, or until slightly browned. Turn the vegetables a couple times during cooking.

3. Remove vegetables from oven and arrange the tofu slices on top the vegetables, with the chermoula side on top. Return pan to the oven to bake for another10 to 15 minutes, or until the tofu is browned.

4. Separate the tofu and vegetables into four plates and serve warm.

Flageolet Bean and Lamb Stew

Preparation time: less than 30 minutes

Cooking time: 1 to 2 hours

Servings: 4

This comforting stew is wonderfully satisfying to curl up with on a cold night. Although it takes a bit longer to cook than some other recipes, this simple one-pot supper will reward you for your time investment.

As part of an intermittent fasting diet plan, 1 serving of flageolet bean and lamb stew provides your 1 allowed daily salty food, and 1/2 (3 out of 6) of your daily recommended servings ofvegetables. This dish contains 290 calories per serving.

Ingredients

- 1 tsp cooking oil
- 12 oz cubed lamb
- 16 pickled onions
- 1 crushed clove of garlic clove

- 20 oz lamb stock
- 8 oz cannedchopped tomatoes
- 1bouquet garni (bundle of herbs)

- ♦ 2 14 oz cans flageolet beans, rinsed and strained
- ♦ 11 oz green beans
- ♦ 9 oz cherry tomatoes
- ♦ Black pepper

Preparation

1. Warm the olive oil in acasserole or saucepan. Add the cubed lamb and stir while cooking for about 3-5 minutes, or until slightly browned all over. Take the lamb out of the casserole or saucepanand set aside.

2. Fry the garlic and onions in the pan for about 4-5 minutes or until onions begin to brown.

3. Add the lamb back into the pan with the garlic and onions. Add the lamb stock, tomatoes, bouquet garni/bundle of herbs and flageolet beans.Bring to a boil and stir,then cover and allow to simmer for 1 hour or until the meat is tender.

4. While this is cooking, boil a pan of water and blanch the green beans. Set aside in bowlof cold water.

5. Add the cherry tomatoes to the stew and season with black pepper. Simmer for another 10 minutes.

6. Ladle the stew onto four plates with the green beans as a side and serve.

TIP:

Because it stores well and has a longer cooking time this is a good recipe to double and save in the freezer or refrigerator for leftovers. In fact, giving the juices and flavors more time to mingle could make the leftover serving even better than the first.

Coriander and Chili Fish Parcel

Preparation time: 1 to 2 hours

Cooking time: less than 30 minutes

Servings: 1

Baking instead of frying fish is an easy method to cut calories. The coriander and chili give this dish a special kick of flavor. This recipe requires a blender or food processor.

As part of an intermittent fasting diet plan, 1 serving of coriander and chili fish parcel provides 1 of your daily recommended 6 servings of vegetables. This dish contains 150 calories.

Ingredients

- 4 oz cod or haddock fillet
- 2 tsp lemon juice
- 1 tbsp coriander leaves
- 1 chopped clove of garlic
- 1 chopped green chili, with the seeds removed
- ¼ tsp sugar
- 2 tsp Greek yogurt
- 3oz steamed snow peas

Preparation

1. Put the fish fillet in a non-metallic dish and squeeze the lemon juice on top.Cover and place in therefrigerator to marinatefor about 20 minutes.

2. Combine the coriander leaves, green chili, and garlic in your food processor or blender or food and mix until it has a paste-like texture. Add in the Greek yogurt and sugar and blend again.

3. Place the fish fillet on a sheet of aluminum foil. Spread the blended paste onto both sides of the fish. Fold the foil loosely and seal at the top. Refrigerate againfor at least 1 hour to marinate.

4. Whilethe fish ismarinating, preheat oven to 400 degrees Fahrenheit. After marinating, take the parcel out of the refrigeratorand place on a baking sheet or pan. Bake the parcel for about 15 minutes, or until the fish is completely cooked through. Arrange on a plate with the steamed snow peas on the side and serve.

Zucchini Tagliatelle with Italian Meatballs

Preparation time: less than 30 minutes

Cooking time: less than 30 minutes

Servings: 2

This tasty dish replaces noodles with zucchini ribbons to create a healthier and lower-calorie version of traditional spaghetti and meatballs.

As part of an intermittent fasting diet plan, 1 serving of zucchini tagliatelle with Italian meatballs provides ½ (3 out of 6) of your recommended daily servings of vegetables. This dish contains 220 calories per serving.

Ingredients

- For meatballs:

- 9 oz extra lean ground beef (make sure it contains 5% fat or less)

- 1 finely chopped onion

- 1 tsp mixed dried herbs

- Cooking spray

- 1 crushed clove of garlic

- 8 oz can chopped tomatoes

- 2 tbsp shredded basil leaves, plus extra for garnishing

- For zucchini tagliatelle:

- 2 zucchinis

- Sea salt

- Black pepper

Preparation

1. Combine ground beef, half of the chopped onion, half of the mixed driedherbs, and a pinch of ground salt and pepper in a bowl. Roll into 10 little balls.

2. Coat a medium non-stick frying pan with cooking oil spray and fry the meatballs for about 5-7 minutes, making sure to turn until browned on all sides. Place meatballs on a plate.

3. For the sauce, put the rest of the chopped onion in the same frying pan and stir over low heat for about 3 minutes, then add the garlic.

4. Add the tomatoes, about 10 oz water, the remaining mixed dried herbs, and the shredded basil leaves.Bring the sauce to a boil and stir.

5. Return the meatballs to the pan with the sauce.Lower the heat to a simmer and stirfor 20 minutes or until the sauce thickens and the meatballs are cooked through.

6. While the meatballs and sauce are cooking, fill a medium pan halfway with water and bring to a boil. Use a potato peeler or a spiralizer if you have one to peel the zucchini into ribbons. Boil the zucchini for 1 minute and then drain.

7. Separate the boiled zucchini ribbons onto two plates and ladle the meatballs and sauce on top. Sprinkle with extra shredded basil leaves to garnish and serve hot.

TIP:

This meal is great for doubling the ingredients to make leftovers. Instead of boiling the zucchini ribbons, you can fry them in a pan for about 1 minute if you prefer. This could make the texture of the zucchini a little firmer than boiling.

Ginger and Soy Sauce Stir-Fried Pork

Preparation time: less than 30 minutes

Cooking time: less than 30 minutes

Servings: 2

This stir-fry dish is a quick and easy lunch or dinner packed with tons of flavor and nutrients.

As part of an intermittent fasting diet plan, 1 serving of ginger and soy sauce stir-fried pork provides your 1 daily allowed salty food, ½ (3 out of 6) of your recommended daily servings of vegetables. The lamb provides plenty of protein and the ginger boosts nutrition with antioxidants. This dish contains 250 calories per serving.

Ingredients

- 9 oz pork tenderloin with visible fat removed and cut into chunks

- 1 tsp corn flour

- 2 tbsp soy sauce

- Cooking spray

- 5 oz sliced button mushrooms

- 2 sliced red peppers

- 2 oz snow peas

- ½ oz fresh root ginger, cut into thin sticks

- 1 sliced clove of garlic

- 4 chopped spring onions

- Black pepper

Preparation

1. Grind black pepperover the porkchunks to taste.Mix the corn flour with two tablespoons of cold water in a small bowl and stir until smooth. Stir in the soy sauce and set aside.

2. Coat a deep-frying pan or large wok with cooking spray oil and place on high heat. Stir-fry the pork for 2 minutes, or until slightly browned but not completely cooked. Move the pork from the frying pan onto a plate.

3. Coat the pan with more cooking spray oil and place over medium to high heat. Stir-fry the mushrooms and peppers fora couple of minutes.Add the snow peas and cook for anotherminute. Add the ginger, garlic, and spring onions and stir just for a few seconds.

4. Add the pork back to the pan or wok and pour over the bowl of soy sauce mixture on top. Stir while cooking for a couple of minutes, or until the sauce is thick and the pork is cooked all the way through. Serve hot.

TIPS:

You can substitute different proteins into this dish, such as lamb, fish, chicken, duck, or tofu.

Garlic and Tomato Shrimp

Preparation time: less than 30 minutes

Cooking time: less than 10 minutes

Servings: 2

This spicy dish of shrimp, garlic, and tomatoes is perfect for heating up a hot summer night or for snuggling up with on a cold winter night. You can adjust the spiciness by adding more or less chili flakes or leaving them out entirely.

As part of an intermittent fasting diet plan, 1 serving of garlic and tomato shrimp provides 1/3 (2 out of 6) of your recommended daily servings of vegetables. This meal contains 180 calories per serving.

Ingredients

- 1 tbsp cooking oil
- 2 sliced cloves of garlic
- 1 chopped red chili OR ½ tsp dried chili flakes
- 5 oz cherry tomatoes cut into halves
- ½ lemon (for juice only)
- 9 oz cooked, peeled, and deveined jumbo shrimp,

- ◆ 3 tbsp chopped parsley leaves
- ◆ Black pepper
- ◆ 6 oz steamed green beans

Preparation

1. Warm the cooking oil in a small frying pan over low heat.Add the garlic and chilior chili flakesand cook for 5 minutes or until the garlic is soft, stirring gently.

2. Add the cherry tomatoes and squeeze the lemon juice, then cook for 2 more minutes or until tomatoes soften. Add the shrimp cook for about 2-3 minutes while stirring, until the tomatoes are completely softened, and the shrimp are cooked all the way through.

3. Remove pan from heat and add in the parsley. Stir and season with ground black pepper. Arrange onto two plates with the steamed green beans as a side and serve hot.

TIP:

You can substitute a different vegetable for the snow peas to add variety to the dish. You can also sprinkle some chili flakes, lemon juice, salt, and pepper over the side vegetable to tie the flavors together.

Stuffed Mushrooms

Preparation time: less than 30 minutes

Cooking time: less than 30 minutes

Servings: 1

This tasty dish is perfect for mushroom lovers. These are great for either lunch, dinner, or a snack.

As part of an intermittent fasting diet plan, 1 serving of stuffed mushrooms provides 1/3 (2 out of 6) of your recommended daily servings of vegetables. This meal contains about 360 calories per serving.

Ingredients

- ♦ 3 Portobello mushrooms
- ♦ 4 oz low-fat ricotta cheese
- ♦ 1.5 oz low-fat grated cheddar cheese
- ♦ 1 oz diced ham
- ♦ 1/4 cup chopped fresh parsley
- ♦ 1ozdiced red pepper

Preparation

1. Preheat your oven to 350 degrees Fahrenheit. Remove and dice the stems of the Portobello mushrooms, then place the mushroom caps on an oven-safe pan or baking sheet lined with foil. This will make cleanup easier as the mushroom caps will release water while cooking. Combine the ham, peppers, parsley, ricotta cheese and diced mushroom stems in a bowl and stir together. Spoon this mixture into the mushroom caps and sprinkle with the grated cheddar cheese.

2. Cook the mushrooms for 20 minutes, or until the mushrooms are slightly browned and the cheese is bubbled.

Rice Cake Caprese

Preparation time: less than 10 minutes

No cooking required

Servings: 1

Vegetarian

This low-calorie snack is high in protein and will keep you full and satisfied. Traditional caprese salad contains mozzarella, but this recipe substitutes cottage cheese for a higher protein, lower calorie version. Have one for a snack or have two or three for a meal. This recipe requiresa mortar and pestle or a food processor. This recipe is for one rice cake, so if you plan to make more than one (you will probably want to!) then multiply the ingredients by the number of rice cakes you want to prepare.

As part of an intermittent fasting diet plan, 1 rice cake caprese provides 1 of your daily servings of dairy. It also has plenty of protein from the cottage cheese and antioxidants from the garlic. This snack contains about 50 calories per serving.

Ingredients

- 1 rice cake
- 2 grape tomatoes or 4 cherry tomatoes, cut into halves
- ½ tsp basil leaves
- ½ tsp garlic
- 1 tbsp low-fat cottage cheese

Preparation

1. Combine the basil and garlic in a food processor, or mash together using a mortar and pestle. If they have trouble mashing into a paste, add a few drops of olive oil. You can multiply the ingredients and make more than one serving and store in the refrigerator.

2. Spread cottage cheese over the rice cake, covering the entire surface. Arrange the halved tomatoes on top. Spoon the basil and garlic mixture on top of the tomatoes and serve.

TIP:

There are lots of ways to mix up this recipe! You could use a slice of fresh mozzarella instead of cottage cheese, or pesto instead of the basil and garlic mixture. You could also sprinkle pine nuts or hemp seeds. Note that any changes will affect the number of calories.

Pesto Tuna Salad

Preparation time: less than 30 minutes

No cooking required

Servings: 1

This delightful pesto tuna salad is rich and creamy, yet still low-calorie. The pesto packs a punch of flavor while the Greek yogurt keeps it light and fresh without feeling too heavy. This low-carb salad if simple and fast to make, and is a great option for lunch, dinner, or even a side salad.

As part of an intermittent fasting diet plan, 1 serving of pesto tuna salad rice provides 1 of your daily servings of dairy, and 1/3 (2 out of 6) of your daily recommended servings of vegetables. It also has plenty of protein from the tuna and Greek yogurt. This salad is also high in magnesium, potassium, and healthy fats. This dish contains about 400 calories per serving.

Ingredients

For tuna:

- ♦ 4 oz can tuna in oil
- ♦ 1 tbsp mayonnaise
- ♦ 1 tbsp Greek yogurt
- ♦ 1 tbsp pesto
- ♦ 2 tspfresh lemon juice
- ♦ Pinch of sea salt

For dressing:

- ♦ 1 tbsp olive oil
- ♦ 1/2 tbsp lemon juice or apple cider vinegar
- ♦ Sea salt
- ♦ Black pepper
- ♦ For salad:
- ♦ 4 shredded leaves iceberg lettuce
- ♦ 1 sliced tomato
- ♦ 1/2 sliced cucumber
- ♦ 1/4 sliced avocado

Preparation

1. To make the tuna, combine all ingredients listed for the tuna and mix with a fork in a bowl.

2. To make the dressing, combine all ingredients listed for the dressing in a jar or any sealed container and shake to combine. You make multiply the ingredients to make extra and store in the refrigerator in a sealed container for up to 4 days.

3. Arrange the lettuce, cucumber, and tomato in a shallow bowl. You can layer or toss them together. Spoon the tuna mixture on top and arrange the avocado slices on top of the tuna. Drizzle with dressing and serve.

TIP:

For an even healthier option, you can make your own mayonnaise out of egg, mustard, white wine vinegar, lemon juice, canola oil, and salt. You can also make your own pesto out of basil, garlic, olive oil, pine nuts, lemon juice, and salt and pepper.

Salmon and Tabbouleh Bowl

Preparation time: less than 30 minutes

Cooking time: 30 minutes

Servings: 2

This salmon and tabbouleh bowl are perfect for a large, healthy meal. It can be eaten for breakfast, lunch, or dinner and is full of flavor and nutrients. It has tons of vegetables, healthy fats, and electrolytes to support an intermittent fasting diet and keep you full for longer.

As part of an intermittent fasting diet plan, 1 serving of this salmon and tabbouleh bowl provides 1 of your daily servings of dairy, and 1/2 (3 out of 6) of your daily recommended servings of vegetables. It also has plenty of protein from the fish, feta cheese and Greek yogurt. This dish is high in magnesium, potassium, and healthy fats, and contains about 400 calories per serving.

Ingredients

For salmon and tabbouleh:

- 2 10 oz salmon fillet
- Sea salt
- Black pepper
- 1 tbsp olive oil
- 9 oz cauliflower
- 1/2 cup redcabbage with the leaves shredded
- 1/4 cup sugar snap peas,chopped
- 1/3 cup chopped red pepper
- 1/4 diced red onion
- 1/4 cup chopped fresh parsley
- 2 tbsp chopped mint
- 1/2 cup crumbled feta cheese
- 3 tbsp olive oil
- 2 tsp fresh lemon juice

For dressing:

- 1 tbsp Greek yogurt
- 1 tbsp chopped basil
- 1 tsp lemon juice
- Sea salt
- Black pepper

Preparation

1. Line a baking sheet or shallow pan with foil and preheat oven to 350 degrees Fahrenheit. Use the salt, pepper, and 1 tsp of olive oil to season the salmon. Put the salmon with the skin facing up on the baking sheet lined with foil and cook in the oven for 25 minutes or until cooked through and the skin is browned and flaky. You could also fry the salmon in a frying pan for a quicker method, if preferred.

2. Chop the cauliflower with a knife or a food processor until it has the consistency of rice. This will be the base of your bowl. Put the cauliflower in a microwave-safe bowl and microwave on high for 4 minutes. You do not need to add water, as water will release naturally form the cauliflower as it heats. Remove from microwave and allow to cool. You may strain the cauliflower rice at this time if you'd like. Fluff the cooled cauliflower with a fork.

3. In another bowl, combine the chopped red cabbage, sugar snap peas, red onion, red pepper, and chopped herbs and toss together.

4. In a separate bowl mix the 2 teaspoons of olive oil, lemon juice, and saltand pepper. Add this olive oil mixture and half of the feta cheese to the cauliflower rice and toss to combine.

5. Combine the ingredients listed for the basil yogurt dressing together in a small bowl.

6. Place the tabbouleh salad on top of the cauliflower rice. Top with your roasted salmon and the remaining feta cheese. Drizzle with the basil yogurt dressing and serve.

TIP:

This dish is best served fresh but can be stored cold for 3 days.

Green Soup with Halloumi Croutons

Preparation time: less than 30 minutes

Cooking time: less than 30 minutes

Servings: 4

Vegetarian

This vibrant green vegetarian soup is deceptively delicious. The mixture of pesto, cream, and halloumi combines creamy, fresh, and salty flavors together that make this soup into a dish that tastes decadent, but it extraordinarily healthy and great for in intermittent fasting diet. It is a highly nutrient-dense meal. You will need a blender for this recipe.

As part of an intermittent fasting diet plan, 1 serving of green soup with halloumi croutons provides 1 of your daily servings of dairy, and 1/2 (3 out of 6) of your daily recommended servings of vegetables. It also has 21 grams of protein, and is high in magnesium, potassium, and healthy fats. This soup contains 300 calories per serving.

Ingredients

For soup:

- 2 tbsp extra virgin olive oil

- 1 diced yellow onion

- 3 minced cloves of garlic

- 5 oz baby spinach

- 8 oz kale

- 1 1/2 cups chopped broccoli

- 1 cup chopped cauliflower

- Pinch of ground cinnamon

- 5 cups (1.2 liters? chicken or vegetable stock

- 1/4 cup almond meal

- 1 tbsp lemon juice

- 2 tbsp heavy whipping cream

- Sea salt

- Black pepper

Topping:

- 1 tbsp extra virgin olive oil

- 5.5 oz diced halloumi cheese

- 4 tbsp pesto

- 4 tbsp heavy whipping cream

Preparation

1. Heat olive oil in a large saucepan over medium heat. Put the garlic and onion in the saucepan, then reduce the heat and cook for 5 minutes or until the onion softens and turns clear.

2. Add the broccoli, cauliflower, kale, and cinnamon to the saucepan. Slowly pour in the stock and then increase the heat again back to medium.

3. Cover saucepan and simmer for 25 minutes, or until all vegetables turn soft. Add in the spinach in the last 5 minutes of cooking.

4. Remove the saucepan from stove and cool a little, but not completely. Add the almond meal, lemon juice, and heavy cream.

5. Blend the mixture in a blender. Season with salt and pepper to taste.

6. For the halloumi croutons, cut the halloumi cheese into bite-sized squares. Add the 1 tbsp ofolive oil to afrying pan and warm over medium to high heat. Fry the halloumi cheese squares and flip to cook both sides as each side browns. Remove from heat.

7. Separate the blended soup into 4 bowls. Swirl each bowl with 1 tbsp of cream and 1 tbsp pesto and top each with 1/4 of thehalloumi croutons and serve.

TIP:

This soup can be stored for up to 5 days in the refrigerator. You can freeze the soup for up to 2 months, but not the halloumi croutons. If you reheat the soup, remember to top with cream, pesto, and croutons before serving.

Chorizo, Chicken and Avocado Salad

Preparation time: less than 30 minutes

Cooking time: less than 30 minutes

Servings: 2

Chicken and chorizo pair wonderfully together with creamy avocado and a delicious homemade dressing to make this filling and healthy salad. It has just the right kick of spice and creaminess to delight your taste buds, and enough nutrients to keep you full until it's time to break your fast.

As part of an intermittent fasting diet plan, 1 serving of chorizo, chicken and avocado salad provides 1 of your daily servings of dairy, and 1/2 (3 out of 6) of your daily recommended servings of vegetables. It also has 43 grams of protein, and is high in magnesium, potassium, and healthy fats. This salad contains 400 calories per serving.

Ingredients

♦ 2 chicken breasts

♦ 1 tsp coconut oil

♦ 2 oz chorizo sausage

♦ 1 diced red onion

♦ 1 cup sugar snap peas

♦ 1/2 avocado

- ♦ 3 tbsp pine nuts
- ♦ 2 tsp olive oil, separated
- ♦ 1/2 tbsp red wine vinegar
- ♦ 1 tbsp soy sauce or coconut aminos
- ♦ 1 tbsp capers
- ♦ .5 oz parsley with the stalks removed
- ♦ .5 oz coriander with the stalks removed
- ♦ 2 tbsp mint leaves
- ♦ 2 tbsp chopped chives
- ♦ Sea salt
- ♦ Black pepper

Preparation

1. Season chicken breasts with salt and pepper and 1 teaspoon of the oil.

2. Coat a frying pan with the coconut oil and set over low to medium heat. Fry the chicken breasts for about 4 minutes on each side, or until the chicken is cooked completely through. Remove chicken from pan and allow to cool. After chicken cools, slice in halves or chop into bite-sized pieces.

3. While the chicken cools, chop the chorizo into bite-sized chunks and fry on low to medium heat for about 2 minutes, or until the oils release. If you are using raw chorizo, cook for longer until the meat is completely cooked through.

4. Add 1 tbsp of olive oil to a clean saucepan and cook the onion on low to medium heat for about 5 minutes, or until soft. Remove from heat, add in the red wine vinegar and coconut aminos/soy sauce, and stir. Add the chorizo, including ant juices or oils.

5. Fill a pan with water and bring to a boil. Blanch the sugar snap peas for 1 minute and then place immediatelyin cold water. Remove from the water and slice the sugar snap peas in half.

6. Chop the herbs and combine by tossing together into a serving bowl. Add the sugar snap peas and the chorizo and onion mixture and arrange the sliced avocado, chicken, pine nuts on top. Add ground salt and pepper to taste and serve.

Disclaimer

The author's ideas and opinions contained in this publication serve to educate the reader in a helpful and informative manner. We accept the instructions may not suit every reader and we expect the recipes not to gel with everyone. The book is to be used responsibly and at your own risk. The provided information in no way guarantees correctness, completion, or quality. Always check with your medical practitioner should you be unsure whether to follow a low carb eating plan. Complete elimination of all misinformation or misprints is not possible. Human error is not a myth!

Imprint

Made in the USA
Middletown, DE
27 July 2019